ETERNAL LIFE AFTER THE STORM

A BOOK OF A CHRISTIAN'S JOURNEY FROM BIRTH TO ETERNAL LIFE

Robert L Shepherd Jr.

Author's Tranquility Press
MARIETTA, GEORGIA

Robert L Shepherd Jr./Author's Tranquility Press
2706 Station Club Drive SW
Marietta, Ga 30060
www.authorstranquilitypress.com

Publisher's Note: This is a work of fiction. Names, characters, places, and inci-dents are a product of the author's imagination. Locales and public names are sometimes used for atmospheric purposes. Any resemblance to actual people, living or dead, or to businesses, companies, events, institutions, or locales is completely coincidental.

Ordering Information:
Quantity sales. Special discounts are available on quantity purchases by cor-porations, associations, and others. For details, contact the "Special Sales De-partment" at the address above.

Eternal Life After the Storm/Robert L Shepherd Jr.
Paperback: 978-1-956480-01-6
eBook: 978-1-956480-02-3

I once again dedicate this book to my lovely wife, Tammara Denise Shepherd, who has endured 38 years as my shipmate on the sea of life as we have navigated and endured the storms before reaching the eternal shore where Jesus awaits with open arms and Eternal Life.

GOD SAW THAT I WAS LONELY
SO HE CREATED YOU FOR ME
AND MOLDED US TOGETHER
FOR ALL THE WORLD TO SEE,
THAT WHAT GOD JOINS TOGETHER,
No rain, wind or thunder,
Man or devil in hell,
Can ever put asunder...

INTRODUCTION

The Christian named Job, who was a contemporary and lived during the time of **Abraham,** cried out, *"Though He slay me, yet will I trust in HIM."*

Job was laying in dust and wallowing in sackcloth and in ashes, scraping himself with **broken-pottery** to relieve himself of some of the irritation and pain he was suffering from being covered in **sore-boils** and eaten alive by **maggots** which thrived and ate upon the decaying skin and sores of his **emaciated flesh.**

Job also being afflicted, responded **in-hope**, envisioning **eternal life** and said, *"And though after my skin worms destroy this body, yet in my flesh shall I see God."*

The **apostle Paul**, who suffered many things himself, said these words to encourage us: *"Therefore we do not lose heart. Even though our outward man is perishing, yet the inward man is renewed day by day."*

"For many", **King David** observed, *"are the afflictions of the righteous: but the LORD delivereth him out of them all."*

This book is written in the year of our LORD, **2021**, to encourage Christians to endure the storms of life**... for Storms must come.**

In this book, I obediently encourages God's people **"to stand!!!"**

"And after having done-all to stand," I encouraged them *"**to keep standing.**"*

1

This **book** is written to encourage faithful **men** and **women** to **endure the storms** in these perilous-last days, before the return of our **Lord Jesus Christ** in **the air**, surrounded by clouds, at the sound of the **angelic trumpet** which only **those who believe** will be able to hear.

In the book of **Job—Job** informs us that *"a man that is born of a woman, live but a few days and those days are full of trouble."*

Hope you enjoy and be blessed by this book!!!

*As you patiently **persevere**,* on planet earth, preparing yourself for everlasting <u>Eternal life</u>, AFTER THE STORM.

DEDICATION

O nce again, I dedicate this book to our **LORD** and **Savior** Jesus Christ, who is the **God** of all creation.

And I thank the **Holy Spirit** for using me once again to pen another book.

I also thank my loving companion, for standing by me in this spiritual battle of life for **38 years**.

And I admonishes **Tammara Denise Shepherd**, to continue to endure hardness as a good soldier...

Baby, **Endure the storms**; realizing better days are ahead in the **glory-of-Eternity**...

I pray for every reader of this book to prosper and be blessed...

And I pray that those who read this book, gather *a few nuggets* from this book, **on how** to <u>persevere</u> and <u>thrive in</u> and *through the* **storms of life**.

3

Job's Storm

I will begin **chapter one** of this book by talking about **Job's storm**, which he experienced and endured while he **lived life** on **planet earth** as an **upright-man** who **loved God** and **avoided all-evil**.
This **book** was written to remind both **saint** and **sinner** that in this life we will face **storms**. Not only **storms** of hurricanes and wind, but **storms** of sicknesses, fear and diseases... **storms** of heartaches, disappointments, lost, and undeserved criticism and abuse.

The man **Job** suffered through all of these **storms** and if you're a man, woman, boy or girl on planet earth; born of a woman, you will experience many of these **storms** too.

In the recorded scriptures from the **book of Job** below, you will see the **personal adversary** and **things** which brought about **Job's** climatic **struggles** and violent **storms**.

And you will see **the** growth and promotion this man of faith will finally experience after ***enduring the storms.***

Job chapter 1:

1 *There was a man in the land of Uz, whose name was Job; and that man was perfect and upright, and one that feared God, and eschewed evil.*

² And there were born unto him seven sons and three daughters.

³ His substance also was seven thousand sheep, and three thousand camels, and five hundred yoke of oxen, and five hundred she asses, and a very great household; so that this man was the greatest of all the men of the east.

⁴ And his sons went and feasted in their houses, every one his day; and sent and called for their three sisters to eat and to drink with them.

⁵ And it was so, when the days of their feasting were gone about, that Job sent and sanctified them, and rose up early in the morning, and offered burnt offerings according to the number of them all: for Job said, It may be that my sons have sinned, and cursed God in their hearts. Thus did Job continually.

⁶ Now there was a day when the sons of God came to present themselves before the LORD, and Satan came also among them.

⁷ And the LORD said unto Satan, Whence comest thou? Then Satan answered the LORD, and said, From going to and fro in the earth, and from walking up and down in it.

⁸ And the LORD said unto Satan, Hast thou considered my servant Job, that there is none like him in the earth, a perfect and an upright man, one that feareth God, and escheweth evil?

9 Then Satan answered the LORD, *and said, Doth Job fear God for nought?*

10 Hast not thou made an hedge about him, and about his house, and about all that he hath on every side? thou hast blessed the work of his hands, and his substance is increased in the land.

11 But put forth thine hand now, and touch all that he hath, and he will curse thee to thy face.

12 And the LORD *said unto Satan, Behold, all that he hath is in thy power; only upon himself put not forth thine hand. So Satan went forth from the presence of the* LORD.

13 And there was a day when his sons and his daughters were eating and drinking wine in their eldest brother's house:

14 And there came a messenger unto Job, and said, The oxen were plowing, and the asses feeding beside them:

15 And the Sabeans fell upon them, and took them away; yea, they have slain the servants with the edge of the sword; and I only am escaped alone to tell thee.

16 While he was yet speaking, there came also another, and said, The fire of God is fallen from heaven, and hath burned up the sheep, and the servants, and consumed them; and I only am escaped alone to tell thee.

17 While he was yet speaking, there came also another, and said, The Chaldeans made out three bands, and fell upon the camels, and have carried them away, yea, and slain the servants with the edge of the sword; and I only am escaped alone to tell thee.

18 While he was yet speaking, there came also another, and said, Thy sons and thy daughters were eating and drinking wine in their eldest brother's house:

19 And, behold, there came a great wind from the wilderness, and smote the four corners of the house, and it fell upon the young men, and they are dead; and I only am escaped alone to tell thee.

20 Then Job arose, and rent his mantle, and shaved his head, and fell down upon the ground, and worshipped,

21 And said, Naked came I out of my mother's womb, and naked shall I return thither: the LORD gave, and the LORD hath taken away; blessed be the name of the LORD.

22 In all this Job sinned not, nor charged God foolishly.

Job chapter Two:

1 Again there was a day when the sons of God came to present themselves before the LORD, and Satan came also among them to present himself before the LORD.

2 And the LORD said unto Satan, From whence comest thou? And Satan answered the LORD, and said, From going to and fro in the earth, and from walking up and down in it.

3 And the LORD said unto Satan, Hast thou considered my servant Job, that there is none like him in the earth, a perfect and an upright man, one that feareth God, and escheweth evil? and still he holdeth fast his integrity, although thou movedst me against him, to destroy him without cause.

4 And Satan answered the LORD, and said, Skin for skin, yea, all that a man hath will he give for his life.

5 But put forth thine hand now, and touch his bone and his flesh, and he will curse thee to thy face.

6 And the LORD said unto Satan, Behold, he is in thine hand; but save his life.

7 So went Satan forth from the presence of the LORD, and smote Job with sore boils from the sole of his foot unto his crown.

8 And he took him a potsherd to scrape himself withal; and he sat down among the ashes.

9 Then said his wife unto him, Dost thou still retain thine integrity? curse God, and die.

10 But he said unto her, Thou speakest as one of the foolish women speaketh. What? shall we receive good at the hand of God, and shall we not receive evil? In all this did not Job sin with his lips.

11 Now when Job's three friends heard of all this evil that was come upon him, they came every one from his own place; Eliphaz the Temanite, and Bildad the Shuhite, and Zophar the Naamathite: for they had made an appointment together to come to mourn with him and to comfort him.

12 And when they lifted up their eyes afar off, and knew him not, they lifted up their voice, and wept; and they rent every one his mantle, and sprinkled dust upon their heads toward heaven.

13 So they sat down with him upon the ground seven days and seven nights, and none spake a word unto him: for they saw that his grief was very great.

Job chapter three:

3 *After this opened Job his mouth, and cursed his day.*

² And Job spake, and said,

³ Let the day perish wherein I was born, and the night in which it was said, There is a man child conceived.

⁴ Let that day be darkness; let not God regard it from above, neither let the light shine upon it.

⁵ Let darkness and the shadow of death stain it; let a cloud dwell upon it; let the blackness of the day terrify it.

⁶ As for that night, let darkness seize upon it; let it not be joined unto the days of the year, let it not come into the number of the months.

⁷ Lo, let that night be solitary, let no joyful voice come therein.

⁸ Let them curse it that curse the day, who are ready to raise up their mourning.

⁹ Let the stars of the twilight thereof be dark; let it look for light, but have none; neither let it see the dawning of the day:

¹⁰ Because it shut not up the doors of my mother's womb, nor hid sorrow from mine eyes.

¹¹ Why died I not from the womb? why did I not give up the ghost when I came out of the belly?

¹² Why did the knees prevent me? or why the breasts that I should suck?

13 For now should I have lain still and been quiet, I should have slept: then had I been at rest,

14 With kings and counsellors of the earth, which build desolate places for themselves;

15 Or with princes that had gold, who filled their houses with silver:

16 Or as an hidden untimely birth I had not been; as infants which never saw light.

17 There the wicked cease from troubling; and there the weary be at rest.

18 There the prisoners rest together; they hear not the voice of the oppressor.

19 The small and great are there; and the servant is free from his master.

20 Wherefore is light given to him that is in misery, and life unto the bitter in soul;

21 Which long for death, but it cometh not; and dig for it more than for hid treasures;

22 Which rejoice exceedingly, and are glad, when they can find the grave?

23 Why is light given to a man whose way is hid, and whom God hath hedged in?

24 For my sighing cometh before I eat, and my roarings are poured out like the waters.

²⁵ For the thing which I greatly feared is come upon me, and that which I was afraid of is come unto me.

²⁶ I was not in safety, neither had I rest, neither was I quiet; yet trouble came.

In the above Texts of **chapter one** through **chapter Three**, we learn about **Job's storm** and the devilish forces that brought about this righteous man's pain and dilemma.

If you are a man born of a woman *into this world*, you too must suffer **storms** in life.

But if you are a Christian, ***be of good cheer;*** for you have overcome the world... *For greater is HE that is within you than the people and demons and devils **in the world,** who'll definitely bring about the **storms**.*

GREATER IS HE THAT IS WITHIN YOU than he that is in the world...

So it was with **Job**...

Job prayed every morning for his family, friends and love ones. But in one day, disaster struck... a storm came and destroyed the house where his **10** kids were partying and killed his children.

And Theives and Terrorists came and destroyed and carried off his livestock.

In **one day**, **Job** lost his children, riches, property, fame, and health.

In **one day**, in the life of the man **Job**, many **storms** would come—which were **originated** and was **orchestrated** by **Satan himself.**

Eventually, even Job's wife came to her husband and unwisely advised him to *"curse God and die"*... instructing him to do the very thing which **Satan** wanted him to do and the very thing which Satan had approached **God's Thorne** asserting that he could make **Job** do.

I did not quote chapter **four through chapter 41 of Job** but let me sum up these chapters now:

In **chapter 4 Job's** three friends hears about **Job's <u>sickness</u>, <u>lost</u>,** and **<u>dilemma</u>** and they came to comfort and console him.

For **seven days** these **<u>3</u> so-called** friends fasted... and sat in sackcloth and ashes with this upright man of God.

Unfortunately, they would eventually began to speak; accusing this upright man of **sin**—and accuses him of secretly being **an <u>evil man</u>**.

Finally, a younger man, named **Elihu**, came along and sat with these **<u>3 accusers.</u>** And he give his *sometime sensible* but mostly **unfounded-knowledge** and **fake news,** as helpful advice to **Job** and his friends.

But Job was an upright man who loved God and his family and his fellow man and eschewed or *"avoided evil."*

In **chapter 38, Job** finally encounter God and hears **HIS** voice.

Even though **God** could not and would not reveal all **HE** knew to **HIS** servant, **Job**...   **God's** presence and voice reassured **Job** that he was **a mere-man** but **HE HIMSELF** was an **Omniscient, Omnipotent, Omnipresent** and **Wise God** who **created all things** and **HE** constantly stood by **Job's** side...

After listening to the council and wisdom of God in **Job chapter 38 through Job chapter 41, Job** finally speaks.

Job Chapter 42:

42 Then Job answered the LORD, and said, ²I know that thou canst do every thing, and that no thought can be withholden from thee.

³Who is he that hideth counsel without knowledge? therefore have I uttered that I understood not; things too wonderful for me, which I knew not.

In the **verses above, Job** confirms **God's greatness.** And he repents of his foolish conversations he had **unwisely babbled** to God and his friends...

And **Job** repented of his lack of understanding and of his imprudence in questioning or trying to understand the wisdom of an **All knowing** and **Almighty God** in his limited **mortal-wisdom** and **understanding.**

⁴Hear, I beseech thee, and I will speak: I will demand of thee, and declare thou unto me.

⁵I have heard of thee by the hearing of the ear: but now mine eye seeth thee.

⁶Wherefore I abhor myself, and repent in dust and ashes.

After **listening, speaking-to** and **seeing** God, **Job** repented in dust and ashes, realizing that he himself **was nothing** but God was **Everything**.

⁷ And it was so, that after the LORD had spoken these words unto Job, the LORD said to Eliphaz the Temanite, My wrath is kindled against thee, and against thy two friends: for yehave not spoken of me the thing that is right, as my servant Job hath.

⁸ Therefore take unto you now seven bullocks and seven rams, and go to my servant Job, and offer up for yourselves a burnt offering; and my servant Job shall pray for you: for him will I accept: lest I deal with you after your folly, in that he have not spoken of me the thing which is right, like my servant Job.

⁹ So Eliphaz the Temanite and Bildad the Shuhite and Zophar the Naamathite went, and did according as the LORD commanded them: the LORD also accepted Job.

¹⁰ And the LORD turned the captivity of Job, when he prayed for his friends: also the LORD gave Job twice as much as he had before.

¹¹ Then came there unto him all his brethren, and all his sisters, and all they that had been of his acquaintance before, and did eat bread with him in his house: and they bemoaned him, and comforted him over all the evil that the LORD had brought upon him: every man also gave him a piece of money, and every one an earring of gold.

¹² So the LORD blessed the latter end of Job more than his beginning: for he had fourteen thousand sheep, and six thousand camels, and a thousand yoke of oxen, and a thousand she asses.

13 He had also seven sons and three daughters.

14 And he called the name of the first, Jemima; and the name of the second, Kezia; and the name of the third, Kerenhap-puch.

15 And in all the land were no women found so fair as the daughters of Job: and their father gave them inheritance among their brethren.

16 After this lived Job an hundred and forty years, and saw his sons, and his sons' sons, even four generations.

*17 So **Job** died, being old and full of days.*

After **Job** had lost <u>his children</u>, <u>his property</u> and <u>endured pain</u>, <u>sorrow</u>, <u>sadness</u> and <u>sickness</u> for so many years—God healed, blessed and restored double to **Job**—*giving-back* everything to **Job**: including blessing **Job** with *longevity*.

So God miraculously blessed him and his wife with **10 more** children and **generations** of **grand** and **great grand-children**...

The later end of **Job** was greater than his beginning, after **Job** had patiently **weathered** and **endured** the **storms**.

Job eventually would die in his bed, surrounded by loved ones and friends.

And I am thoroughly convinced that one day, this **man-of-trouble** we read and talk so much about; who **suffered** and **endured** so many **storms** in life-we'll see again in **Eternity** with **Jesus Christ**, rejoicing with **God's children**, of all generations, whom were <u>**born-of-a-woman**</u>, <u>**loved God**</u> and patiently **endured life's storms**.

CHAPTER TWO

The Prophet Jonah's Storm

In **Chapter Two** of this book we will talk about **Jonah the prophet,** who brought about his own **troubles** and **storm;** by neglecting to obey God and to follow **HIS** instructions.

Take close attention and notate **Jonah's** pride, arrogance and disobedient-attitude so that you will not imitate **Jonah** and **tempt God**—thereby creating for yourself unnecessary **storms** and **troubles.**

Jonah: chapter 1

1 Now the word of the LORD came unto Jonah the son of Amittai, saying,

² Arise, go to Nineveh, that great city, and cry against it; for their wickedness is come up before me.

³ But Jonah rose up to flee unto Tarshish from the presence of the LORD, and went down to Joppa; and he found a ship going to Tarshish: so he paid the fare thereof, and went down into it, to go with them unto Tarshish from the presence of the LORD.

In the above verses Jonah receives a direct command from God to go to Nineveh and preach **HIS Word**. But **Jonah** refused too and got on a ship going in the opposite direction to **Tarshish**.

Jonah's disobedience made a **Loving God** angry so God brought about a **storm** that would eventually cause **Jonah** to **repent**; and **cry out** for another chance to do **HIS Will.**

The **point** I want you to get from this chapter is this: **"Our rebellion against God's Word** will always create **storms** in our lives."

⁴ But the L*ORD* *sent out a great wind into the sea, and there was a mighty tempest in the sea, so that the ship was like to be broken.*

In the above text, **Jonah** was sent to evangelize Nineveh but he hated these people and he refused his **God-given assignment** and went another way, provoking **God's wrath** and producing a **sudden-storm** in his life.

⁵ Then the mariners were afraid, and cried every man unto his god, and cast forth the wares that were in the ship into the sea, to lighten it of them. But Jonah was gone down into the sides of the ship; and he lay, and was fast asleep.

⁶ So the shipmaster came to him, and said unto him, What meanest thou, O sleeper? arise, call upon thy God, if so be that God will think upon us, that we perish not.

⁷ And they said every one to his fellow, Come, and let us cast lots, that we may know for whose cause this evil is upon us. So they cast lots, and the lot fell upon Jonah.

⁸ Then said they unto him, Tell us, we pray thee, for whose cause this evil is upon us; What is thine occupation? and whence comest thou? what is thy country? and of what people art thou?

⁹ And he said unto them, I am an Hebrew; and I fear the LORD, *the God of heaven, which hath made the sea and the dry land.*

¹⁰ Then were the men exceedingly afraid, and said unto him. Why hast thou done this? For the men knew that he fled from the presence of the LORD, *because he had told them.*

¹¹ Then said they unto him, What shall we do unto thee, that the sea may be calm unto us? for the sea wrought, and was tempestuous.

¹² And he said unto them, Take me up, and cast me forth into the sea; so shall the sea be calm unto you: for I know that for my sake this great tempest is upon you.

¹³ Nevertheless the men rowed hard to bring it to the land; but they could not: for the sea wrought, and was tempestuous against them.

¹⁴ Wherefore they cried unto the LORD, *and said, We beseech thee, O* LORD, *we beseech thee, let us not perish for this man's life, and lay not upon us innocent blood: for thou, O* LORD, *hast done as it pleased thee.*

¹⁵ So they took up Jonah, and cast him forth into the sea: and the sea ceased from her raging.

*¹⁶ Then the men **feared the** LORD **exceedingly, and offered a sacrifice unto the** LORD**, and made vows.***

¹⁷ Now the LORD *had prepared a great fish to swallow up Jonah. And Jonah was **in the belly of the fish three days** and **three nights.***

Even *through* Jonah's <u>defiant rebellion</u>—the Sovereign God still saved sinners, wrought miracles and fulfilled prophecies.

Jonah: chapter 2

¹ Then Jonah prayed unto the Lord his God out of the fish's belly,

² And said, I cried by reason of mine affliction unto the Lord, and he heard me; out of the belly of hell cried I, and thou heardest my voice.

³ For thou hadst cast me into the deep, in the midst of the seas; and the floods compassed me about: all thy billows and thy waves passed over me.

⁴ Then I said, I am cast out of thy sight; yet I will look again toward thy holy temple.

⁵ The waters compassed me about, even to the soul: the depth closed me round about, the weeds were wrapped about my head.

⁶ I went down to the bottoms of the mountains; the earth with her bars was about me for ever: yet hast thou brought up my life from corruption, O Lord my God.

⁷ When my soul fainted within me I remembered the Lord: and my prayer came in unto thee, into thine holy temple.

⁸ They that observe lying vanities forsake their own mercy.

⁹ But I will sacrifice unto thee with the voice of thanksgiving; I will pay that that I have vowed. Salvation is of the Lord.

¹⁰ And the LORD spake unto the fish, and it vomited out Jonah upon the dry land.

Jonah is given another chance to obey God and do **HIS Will**.

Jonah: chapter 3

1 *And the word of the LORD came unto Jonah the second time, saying,*

² Arise, go unto Nineveh, that great city, and preach unto it the preaching that I bid thee.

³ So Jonah arose, and went unto Nineveh, according to the word of the LORD. Now Nineveh was an exceeding great city of three days' journey.

⁴ And Jonah began to enter into the city a day's journey, and he cried, and said, Yet forty days, and Nineveh shall be overthrown.

⁵ So the people of Nineveh believed God, and proclaimed a fast, and put on sackcloth, from the greatest of them even to the least of them.

⁶ For word came unto the king of Nineveh, and he arose from his throne, and he laid his robe from him, and covered him with sackcloth, and sat in ashes.

⁷ And he caused it to be proclaimed and published through Nineveh by the decree of the king and his nobles, saying, Let neither man nor beast, herd nor flock, taste any thing: let them not feed, nor drink water:

⁸ But let man and beast be covered with sackcloth, and cry mightily unto God: yea, let them turn every one from his evil way, and from the violence that is in their hands.

⁹ Who can tell if God will turn and repent, and turn away from his fierce anger, that we perish not?

¹⁰ And God saw their works, that they turned from their evil way; and God repented of the evil, that he had said that he would do unto them; and he did it not.

After **Jonah** preaches to Nineveh, the whole city humble themselves, **fast** and **pray**, and **seek God's Face** and **turn from their wickedness** and are saved—to **Jonah's** dissatisfaction and disapproval.

Jonah: Chapter Four

1 But it displeased Jonah exceedingly, and he was very angry.

² And he prayed unto the LORD, and said, I pray thee, O LORD, was not this my saying, when I was yet in my country? Therefore I fled before unto Tarshish: for I knew that thou art a gracious God, and merciful, slow to anger, and of great kindness, and repentest thee of the evil.

³ Therefore now, O LORD, take, I beseech thee, my life from me; for it is better for me to die than to live.

⁴ Then said the LORD, Doest thou well to be angry?

⁵ So Jonah went out of the city, and sat on the east side of the city, and there made him a booth, and sat under it in the shadow, till he might see what would become of the city.

⁶ And the LORD God prepared a gourd, and made it to come up over Jonah, that it might be a shadow over his head, to

deliver him from his grief. So Jonah was exceeding glad of the gourd.

7 But God prepared a worm when the morning rose the next day, and it smote the gourd that it withered.

8 And it came to pass, when the sun did arise, that God prepared a vehement east wind; and the sun beat upon the head of Jonah, that he fainted, and wished in himself to die, and said, It is better for me to die than to live.

9 And God said to Jonah, Doest thou well to be angry for the gourd? And he said, I do well to be angry, even unto death.

10 Then said the LORD, Thou hast had pity on the gourd, for the which thou hast not laboured, neither madest it grow; which came up in a night, and perished in a night:

11 And should not I spare Nineveh, that great city, wherein are more than sixscore thousand persons that cannot discern between their right hand and their left hand; and also much cattle?

In the book of Jonah, we learn that our disobedience and refusal to obey God will not only bring **storms** into our lives but will also bring about **storms** and **destruction** and **lost** into the lives of those around us.

We must daily practice to love and serve God...

Our **Loving God** so loved the world that he want every man, **woman**, **boy** and **girl** to repent and be saved to avoid self-created **storms**.

CHAPTER THREE

The Disciples Storm

Matthew 8:23-27:

23 And when he was entered into a ship, his disciples followed him.

24 And, behold, there arose a great tempest in the sea, insomuch that the ship was covered with the waves: but he was asleep.

25 And his disciples came to him, and awoke him, saying, Lord, save us: we perish.

26 And he saith unto them, Why are ye fearful, O ye of little faith? Then he arose, and rebuked the winds and the sea; and there was a great calm.

27 But the men marvelled, saying, What manner of man is this, that even the winds and the sea obey him!

We will always encounter **storms** in this life but we must realize that HE is with us and that through **HIM** we have the power to **rebuke storms,** cast **out devils** and **lay hands on the sick** so that they can **be healed!!!**

Matthew 14: 22-33:

22

28 *And straightway Jesus constrained his disciples to get into a ship, and to go before him unto the other side, while he sent the multitudes away.*

23 *And when he had sent the multitudes away, he went up into a mountain apart to pray: and when the evening was come, he was there alone.*

24 *But the ship was now in the midst of the sea, tossed with waves: for the wind was contrary.*

25 *And in the fourth watch of the night Jesus went unto them, walking on the sea.*

26 *And when the disciples saw him walking on the sea, they were troubled, saying, It is a spirit; and they cried out for fear.*

27 *But straightway Jesus spake unto them, saying, Be of good cheer; it is I; be not afraid.*

28 *And Peter answered him and said, Lord, if it be thou, bid me come unto thee on the water.*

29 *And he said, Come. And when Peter was come down out of the ship, he walked on the water, to go to Jesus.*

30 *But when he saw the wind boisterous, he was afraid; and beginning to sink, he cried, saying, Lord, save me.*

31 *And immediately Jesus stretched forth his hand, and caught him, and said unto him, O thou of little faith, wherefore didst thou doubt?*

³² And when they were come into the ship, the wind ceased.

³³ Then they that were in the ship came and worshipped him, saying, Of a truth thou art the Son of God.

If we use our **faith** when we encounter **storms** in this life while on our journey to the other side, we're see **Jesus** beckoning us to walk on water, thereby seeing **miracles** and **wonders** that only **storms** and faith can produce in our lives.

Mark 4:36-41

³⁶ And when they had sent away the multitude, they took him even as he was in the ship. And there were also with him other little ships.

³⁷ And there arose a great storm of wind, and the waves beat into the ship, so that it was now full.

³⁸ And he was in the hinder part of the ship, asleep on a pillow: and they awake him, and say unto him, Master, carest thou not that we perish?

³⁹ And he arose, and rebuked the wind, and said unto the sea, Peace, be still. And the wind ceased, and there was a great calm.

⁴⁰ And he said unto them, Why are ye so fearful? how is it that ye have no faith?

⁴¹ And they feared exceedingly, and said one to another, What manner of man is this, that even the wind and the sea obey him?

There's nothing impossible for our God to subdue and conquer. We must know and realize this as we face storms that we are sure to unexpectedly encounter in this life.

Our **God** is the sort of **Man** that even the <u>sea</u> and <u>wind</u> and <u>mighty storms</u> must listen to and obey **HIS word**.

Luke 8: 22-25:

²² Now it came to pass on a certain day, that he went into a ship with his disciples: and he said unto them, Let us go over unto the other side of the lake. And they launched forth.

²³ But as they sailed he fell asleep: and there came down a storm of wind on the lake; and they were filled with water, and were in jeopardy.

²⁴ And they came to him, and awoke him, saying, Master, master, we perish. Then he arose, and rebuked the wind and the raging of the water: and they ceased, and there was a calm.

²⁵ And he said unto them, Where is your faith? And they being afraid wondered, saying one to another, What manner of man is this! for he commandeth even the winds and water, and they obey him.

John 6:16-21:

¹⁶ And when even was now come, his disciples went down unto the sea,

¹⁷ of Capernaum. And it was now dark, and Jesus was not come to them.

¹⁸ And the sea arose by reason of a great wind that blew.

19 So when they had rowed about five and twenty or thirty furlongs, they see Jesus walking on the sea, and drawing nigh unto the ship: and they were afraid.

20 But he saith unto them, It is I; be not afraid.

21 Then they willingly received him into the ship: and immediately the ship was at the land whither they went.

Father God, our salvation and security is derived in this life only when we invite Jesus into our heart as **Lord, Forgiver, Holy sacrifice** and as the **Savior** of our **soul**.

 Let's do it now!!!

"*Heavenly Father,* I realize that you're God, the Creator and Savior, so I invite you into my life as my ***LORD and Savior.***

I submit my body, soul and spirit unto *YOU* today *LORD Jesus,* and by personally accepting your **sacrifice** and **death and work on the cross,** and by believing the Father raised you from the dead; I now thank you *Lord* for saving me and delivering me **through** and **from** all of the **storms,** I'll encounter as a **man born of a woman.** *In Jesus Name!*

In this **chapter** entitled **The Disciple Storms,** we too must realize that by following our **Lord Jesus Christ,** we also shall suffer going through **storms** on our journey through life but we must be of *good-cheer, "for we , through our Lord and Savior Jesus Christ—have overcome the world."*

CHAPTER FOUR

Euroclydon

(The Apostle Paul's Storm)

Acts 27:

1 And when it was determined that we should sail into Italy, they delivered Paul and certain other prisoners unto one named Julius, a centurion of Augustus' band.

2 And entering into a ship of Adramyttium, we launched, meaning to sail by the coasts of Asia; one Aristarchus, a Macedonian of Thessalonica, being with us.

3 And the next day we touched at Sidon. And Julius courteously entreated Paul, and gave him liberty to go unto his friends to refresh himself.

4 And when we had launched from thence, we sailed under Cyprus, because the winds were contrary.

5 And when we had sailed over the sea of Cilicia and Pamphylia, we came to Myra, a city of Lycia.

6 And there the centurion found a ship of Alexandria sailing into Italy; and he put us therein.

7 And when we had sailed slowly many days, and scarce were come over against Cnidus, the wind not suffering us, we sailed under Crete, over against Salmone;

8 And, hardly passing it, came unto a place which is called The fair havens; nigh whereunto was the city of Lasea.

9 Now when much time was spent, and when sailing was now dangerous, because the fast was now already past, Paul admonished them,

10 And said unto them, Sirs, I perceive that this voyage will be with hurt and much damage, not only of the lading and ship, but also of our lives.

11 Nevertheless the centurion believed the master and the owner of the ship, more than those things which were spoken by Paul.

12 And because the haven was not commodious to winter in, the more part advised to depart thence also, if by any means they might attain to Phenice, and there to winter; which is an haven of Crete, and lieth toward the south west and north west.

13 And when the south wind blew softly, supposing that they had obtained their purpose, loosing thence, they sailed close by Crete.

14 But not long after there arose against it a tempestuous wind, called Euroclydon.

15 And when the ship was caught, and could not bear up into the wind, we let her drive.

16 And running under a certain island which is called Clauda, we had much work to come by the boat:

17 *Which when they had taken up, they used helps, under-girding the ship; and, fearing lest they should fall into the quicksands, strake sail, and so were driven.*

18 *And we being exceedingly tossed with a tempest, the next day they lightened the ship;*

19 *And the third day we cast out with our own hands the tackling of the ship.*

20 *And when neither sun nor stars in many days appeared, and no small tempest lay on us, all hope that we should be saved was then taken away.*

21 *But after long abstinence Paul stood forth in the midst of them, and said, Sirs, ye should have hearkened unto me, and not have loosed from Crete, and to have gained this harm and loss.*

22 *And now I exhort you to be of good cheer: for there shall be no loss of any man's life among you, but of the ship.*

23 *For there stood by me this night the angel of God, whose I am, and whom I serve,*

24 *Saying, Fear not, Paul; thou must be brought before Cae-sar: and, lo, God hath given thee all them that sail with thee.*

25 *Wherefore, sirs, be of good cheer: for I believe God, that it shall be even as it was told me.*

26 *Howbeit we must be cast upon a certain island.*

27 *But when the fourteenth night was come, as we were driven up and down in Adria, about midnight the shipmen deemed that they drew near to some country;*

28 And sounded, and found it twenty fathoms: and when they had gone a little further, they sounded again, and found it fifteen fathoms.

29 Then fearing lest we should have fallen upon rocks, they cast four anchors out of the stern, and wished for the day.

30 And as the shipmen were about to flee out of the ship, when they had let down the boat into the sea, under colour as though they would have cast anchors out of the foreship,

31 Paul said to the centurion and to the soldiers, **Except these abide in the ship, ye cannot be saved.**

32 Then the soldiers cut off the ropes of the boat, and let her fall off.

33 And while the day was coming on, Paul besought them all to take meat, saying, This day is the fourteenth day that ye have tarried and continued fasting, having taken nothing.

34 Wherefore I pray you to take some meat: for this is for your health: for there shall not an hair fall from the head of any of you.

35 And when he had thus spoken, he took bread, and gave thanks to God in presence of them all: and when he had broken it, he began to eat.

36 Then were they all of good cheer, and they also took some meat.

37 And we were in all in the ship two hundred threescore and sixteen souls.

38 And when they had eaten enough, they lightened the ship, and cast out the wheat into the sea.

39 And when it was day, they knew not the land: but they discovered a certain creek with a shore, into the which they were minded, if it were possible, to thrust in the ship.

40 And when they had taken up the anchors, they committed themselves unto the sea, and loosed the rudder bands, and hoised up the mainsail to the wind, and made toward shore.

41 And falling into a place where two seas met, they ran the ship aground; and the forepart stuck fast, and remained unmoveable, but the hinder part was broken with the violence of the waves.

42 And the soldiers' counsel was to kill the prisoners, lest any of them should swim out, and escape.

43 But the centurion, willing to save Paul, kept them from their purpose; and commanded that they which could swim should cast themselves first into the sea, and get to land:

44 And the rest, some on boards, and some on broken pieces of the ship. And so it came to pass, that they escaped all safe to land.

In **Paul's storm**, as he was going to Rome, for his final destiny and commission to preach the gospel to the Roman gentiles, a great storm called **Euroclydon** suddenly arose to destroy the ship and all of the people in it.

This **storm** could have been avoided if the ship leaders would have only listen to Paul, the prophet and man of God, but they would not.

So many unnecessary storms shall occur in our lives because of others foolish decisions to ignore God and operate in HIS Wisdom and Truth.

So it was in Paul's life: as He journeyed across the **Mediterranean Sea** to **Rome**, for his final ministry and destiny, in his days of living through the **storms**.

When the **souls** on this ship and journey finally began to listen to the **Apostle Paul** as he obediently heard from and obeyed the **Creator** who spoke from heaven; **no soul was lost**—but by holding on to **broken pieces**, as they were instructed to do by the man of God; **all men** on board the wrecked ship were *saved* and *safely reached* **shore**.

EPILOGUE

I wrote this book as a **storm** unsuspectedly and suddenly appeared in my life, causing me to bow to my feeble knees at my reclining chair to call upon the **NAME of the LORD**, beseeching **HIM** for help in a time of trouble.

While tarrying on my knees, a still small voice spoke to me urging me to *"Endure the Storm"* because after the storm is **Eternal Life.**

At that moment, while on my knees, I realized God was calling me to write another book and to share this Truth **HE** was teaching me.

Readers, I have now penned this book **Eternal life after the Storm** and I pray that something said or mentioned in this book will help you to endure your **storms** in this life; which is destined to occur in the lives of every man, woman, boy or girl on planet Earth—**born of a woman**.

My prayer and hope for the readers of this book is for you all, to fix your eyes on the water-walking **JESUS** and daily live in preparation for: **Eternal Life after the Storm!!!**

ABOUT THE AUTHOR

Robert L. Shepherd, Jr. is a poet, writer, and ordained Minister called to teach and inspire the Body of Christ through the Word of God. He is empowered by the Holy Ghost with the Word of wisdom, prophecy, and the Spirit of discernment. For years, brother Shepherd has shared and enlightened numerous souls of God's intended purpose for their lives. "For I know the plans I have for you, declares the Lord, plans to prosper you and not to harm you, plans to give you hope and a future. (Jeremiah 29:11) NIV

CPSIA information can be obtained
at www.ICGtesting.com
Printed in the USA
LVHW111621030922
727557LV00018B/215